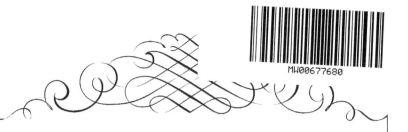

ISBN 978-1-331-01542-0
PIBN 10133787

Forgotten Books is a registered trademark of FB &c Ltd.
Copyright © 2018 FB &c Ltd.
FB &c Ltd, Dalton House, 60 Windsor Avenue, London, SW19 2RR.
Company number 08720141. Registered in England and Wales.

For support please visit www.forgottenbooks.com

1 MONTH OF
FREE
READING

at

www.ForgottenBooks.com

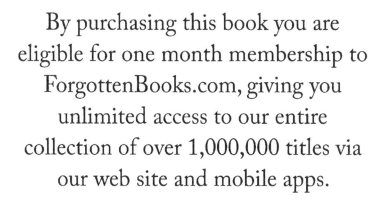

By purchasing this book you are eligible for one month membership to ForgottenBooks.com, giving you unlimited access to our entire collection of over 1,000,000 titles via our web site and mobile apps.

To claim your free month visit:

www.forgottenbooks.com/free133787

English
Français
Deutsche
Italiano
Español
Português

www.forgottenbooks.com

Mythology Photography **Fiction**
Fishing Christianity **Art** Cooking
Essays Buddhism Freemasonry
Medicine **Biology** Music **Ancient**
Egypt Evolution Carpentry Physics
Dance Geology **Mathematics** Fitness
Shakespeare **Folklore** Yoga Marketing
Confidence Immortality Biographies
Poetry **Psychology** Witchcraft
Electronics Chemistry History **Law**
Accounting **Philosophy** Anthropology
Alchemy Drama Quantum Mechanics
Atheism Sexual Health **Ancient History**
Entrepreneurship Languages Sport
Paleontology Needlework Islam
Metaphysics Investment Archaeology
Parenting Statistics Criminology
Motivational

OR A BUSY DAY:

A MORNING PRAYER FOR A BUSY OR TROUBLED WEEK-DAY.

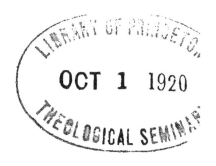

BY

J. R. MILLER, D.D.,

AUTHOR OF "WEEK-DAY RELIGION," "PRACTICAL RELIGION,"
"LIFE'S BYWAYS AND WAYSIDES," ETC., ETC.

PHILADELPHIA:

PRESBYTERIAN BOARD OF PUBLICATION
AND SABBATH-SCHOOL WORK.

1895.

THE sweetest flower needs heaven's sunshine and dew to perfect its beauty and sustain its life. So does the holiest human life need God. A picture without sky in it is incomplete. A day on earth without a glimpse of heaven to brighten it dies without a blessing. We rob our own nature and impoverish our life if we do not avail ourselves of the help and renewal which we may get through prayer. Prayer lifts us into the very presence of God. It brings down upon us the power of Christ, according to the measure of our need and the measure of our faith. He who lives without prayer lives without God. He who lives a life of prayer walks with God by day and by night. The more we have to do, and the more care we have, the more do we need to begin our days with prayer.

"Cause me to hear thy lovingkindness in the morning;
   For in thee do I trust:
Cause me to know the way wherein I should walk;
   For I lift up my soul unto thee.
Deliver me, O Lord, from mine enemies:
   I flee unto thee to hide me.
Teach me to do thy will; for thou art my God:
   Thy spirit is good; lead me in the land of uprightness.
Quicken me, O Lord, for thy name's sake:
   In thy righteousness bring my soul out of trouble."

PSALM cxliii: 8–11.

"When first the eyes unveil, give thy soul leave
   To do the like; our bodies but forerun
The spirit's duty. True hearts spread and heave
   Unto their God, as flowers do to the sun.
Give him thy first thought then; so shalt thou keep
Him company all day, and in him sleep."

HENRY VAUGHAN.

FOR A BUSY DAY.

NO day starts well without its morning prayer. We need to get the touch of Christ's hand upon us to give us calmness and strength as we go forth. There is a story of a Christian woman whose life was full of tasks and cares. One morning she had been unusually hurried in getting her household ready for the day, and she had not kept quiet and sweet through it all. She had lost patience and had become fretted and vexed. Her heart had been in a fever of disquiet all the morning.

When the children were off for school and the pressing tasks were finished, the tired woman went to her own room. She was discouraged. The day had begun most unsatisfactorily. She took up her Bible and read the story of the healing of the sick woman: " He touched her hand, and the fever left her; and she arose, and ministered unto them."

"If I could have had that cooling, healing touch on my hand," she said, "before I began my morning's work, the fever would have left me, too, and then I could have ministered sweetly to my household." She had learned that the first touch in the morning should be Christ's. We need his healing before we are ready for any true serving.

This is especially true of our week-days. We can get along better on Sunday. The air is clearer and heaven seems nearer. We rest from the tasks and toils which ofttimes so fill and overfill our hands on the other days. We do not have to go out into the noisy world to endure its frictions and strifes, and take part in its rivalries and competitions. We can stay at home, in love's quiet shelter, on the Sabbath, and go to God's house, which is a sanctuary for our souls, a quiet and still resting-place. It is not so hard for most of us to live sweetly and victoriously on Sunday.

But the week-days try us. Many of us have to rise early and hurry away to work which is ofttimes hard and which sometimes irks us. Perhaps we are thrown among people who are not kindly and congenial, who sorely try us and sometimes fret us by their spirit that is unrefined, their talk that is distasteful, and their conduct that is unseemly. Perhaps the days bring their temptations, requiring us to be continually under sore restraint, lest we yield and say words we ought not to say. It may be that the grinding pressure of the day is too great for our strength, that the burdens are too heavy, the tasks too hard, the hours too long. Some of us must work under masters who are not always gentle and thoughtful, who exact more than is just, and who are lacking in sympathy and human feeling. Some of us have to contend all the day with discouraging conditions in business, meeting losses and sustaining reverses.

It is our week-days that test us. Many of us find it much harder to keep sweet and patient and at peace then than on the quiet Sabbaths. Then we are within the gates of the refuge, with the dangers and troubles shut out; on the week-days we are out in the open, unsheltered field, where storms beat and suns smite and perils sweep unhindered. The Sabbaths are oases, with their wells of water and their palm-trees; the week-days are desert, with waterless sands, shadeless stretches, and hot simooms.

In an old psalm there is a prayer that is most fitting for the morning of a busy week-day. It is not new; but human hearts change not, human needs are the same in all centuries, and therefore this prayer which no doubt brought blessing to a struggling life, when first offered long ago, may bring blessing into struggling lives any of these modern days. The prayer runs thus:

" Cause me to hear thy lovingkindness in the morning;
For in thee do I trust:
Cause me to know the way wherein I should walk;
For I lift up my soul unto thee.
Deliver me, O Lord, from mine enemies:
I flee unto thee to hide me.
Teach me to do thy will; for thou art my God:
Thy spirit is good; lead me in the land of uprightness.
Quicken me, O Lord, for thy name's sake:
In thy righteousness bring my soul out of trouble."

If we will make this prayer our own, it will bring blessing and peace into our heart through the most troubled week-days. There are six petitions in the prayer.

I. TO HEAR GOD'S VOICE FIRST.

"Cause me to hear thy lovingkindness in the morning; for in thee do I trust." This is a prayer that the first voice to break upon our ear at the opening of the day shall be the voice of God, speaking in love. We ought to try to see Christ's face before we look upon any human face, when we awake in the morning. Professor Drummond says, " Five minutes spent in the companionship of Christ, every morning,—aye, two minutes, if it be face to face and heart to heart,—will change your whole day, will make every thought and feeling different, will enable you to do things for his sake that you would not have done for your own sake, or for any one's sake."

Perhaps not sufficient use is made of the Bible in the ordinary devotions of Christian people. It is not enough to speak to God, telling him of our wants, our dangers, our sins, our troubles, and to plead with him for help, for favor, for comfort. We must also let God speak to us, and we must be quiet that we may hear what he has to say. We must feed our souls on the holy Word. No exercise of devotion is complete without the reading of some sentence or sentences which will start in our minds inspiring thoughts. If nothing more is possible, we should take at least a verse for the day. This will prove a benediction through all the hours. It will start a song in our heart, in the early morning, which will go singing till nightfall. It will bring a fragment of heaven down into our common life, to brighten it, and to become impulse, cheer, comfort, encouragement, and hope for us when cares and duties grow burdensome. It will give us a definite lesson to master for the day, set a standard before us toward which to strive, speak to us a word of counsel to make the way plainer for our feet, and become a lamp to shine on our path to show us how to walk.

Then it is sweet to look into Christ's face in the first waking moment, to thank him for his love, to receive his smile of forgiveness and peace and his benediction for the day. It prepares us for duty. It gives us fresh courage. "They that wait upon the Lord shall renew their strength." After our little time with God in the morning we are ready for anything the day may bring, and need dread no possible exprience.

"One hour with thee, my God, when daylight breaks
   Over a world thy guardian care has kept;
When the fresh soul from soothing slumber wakes
   To praise the love that watched me while I slept;
When with new strength my blood is bounding free,
The first, best, sweetest hour I'll give to thee.

"One hour with thee when busy day begins
   Her never-ceasing round of bustling care;
When I must meet with toil, and pain, and sins,
   And through them all thy holy cross must bear,
Oh, then, to arm me for the strife,—to be
Faithful to death,—I'll kneel one hour with thee!"

It was said that when the rays of morning broke over the plains of ancient Egypt, the harp of Memnon, held in the hands of the famous statue at Thebes, poured out soft, sweet music on the air. The waves of morning light made the music, as they swept gently over the chords of the harp. When the beams of God's loving-kindness touch our hearts at the early dawn, they should start songs of gladness, joy, and peace.

A strange instrument hung on an old castle wall,—so the legend runs. No one knew how to use it. Its strings were broken and covered with the dust of many years. Those who looked at the instrument wondered what it was and what purpose it had served. One day a stranger came to the castle gate and entered the hall. His eye noted the harp on the wall, and, taking it down, he reverently brushed away the dust and tenderly reset the broken strings. The chords long silent woke beneath his skilful touch, and all who heard the music were thrilled by it. It was the master, long absent, who had come back again to his castle.

It is only a legend, but it is a legend with a meaning. In every human soul there hangs a marvellous harp, dust-covered, with strings jangled and broken, until the Master comes and with his own hand mends the broken harp and strikes it with his own fingers.

> "Ah, could the tender Christ but brush away,
> And o'er the slumbering tones his fingers sweep,
> A world would pause to catch the echoing chord
> Of music wakened 'neath the touch of God."

If we would have a day of songful life we must open our heart every morning to the Master, Christ. He will repair the strings which sin has broken and put them in tune, and then will sweep them with his skilful fingers. Then we can go forth to experiences of peace and blessing. When the song of God's love is singing in our soul we are ready for the new day.

II. TO KNOW THE WAY.

The second petition of this morning prayer is, "Cause me to know the way wherein I should walk." We cannot know the way ourselves. The path across one little day seems very short, but none of us can find it ourself. Each day is a hidden world to our eyes, as we enter it in the morning. We cannot see one step before us as we go forth. An impenetrable veil covers the brightest day as with night's black robes. It may have joys and prosperities for us, or it may bring to us sorrows and adversities. Our path may lead us into a garden, or the garden may be a Gethsemane. We have our plans as we go out in the morning, but we are not sure that they will be realized. The day will bring duties, responsibilities, temptations, perils, tangles which our fingers cannot unravel, intricate or obscure paths in which we cannot find the way.

What could be more fitting in the morning

than the prayer, " Cause me to know the way wherein I should walk"? God knows all that is in the day for us. His eye sees to its close and he can be our guide. There is no promise given more repeatedly in the Bible than that of divine guidance. We have it in the shepherd psalm, "He leadeth me in the paths of righteousness." Paths of righteousness are right paths. Of course, God will never lead us in any wrong or sinful way. That is one meaning. All God's paths are clean and holy. They are the ways of the commandments. But there is another sense in which they are right paths. They are the right ways, the best ways for us. Ofttimes they are not the ways which we would have chosen. They do not seem to be good ways. But nevertheless they are right, and lead to blessing and honor. We are always safe, therefore, in praying this prayer on the morning of any day: "Cause me to know the way wherein I should walk."

God has many ways of answering this prayer. When we ask him to show us the road, he puts his Word into our hands, and says, "Take, read." The Bible is of use to us only when we read it and ponder its teachings, and then set ourselves to obey it. This suggests again the importance of reading the Bible in our morning devotions. Else how shall we learn what God would say to us in answer to our prayer?

There are other ways. Every good and perfeet gift comes down from the Father. No matter through what source, or at the lips of what messenger, the counsel or the wisdom comes, it is from God. When you are in some perplexity about duty, and pray that God would cause you to know the way in which you should walk, you may find the answer in a book whose words, as you read them, make the way plain and clear to you. Or you may find it in the quiet words of a friend to whom you turn with your question. Happy are the young people who, in their days of inexperience, when all life is yet new, have a wise older friend to whom they may go with perfect trust with the questions that must always arise. Far more than we realize does God show us the way through human guides. He thus hides himself in the love and wisdom of those who are dear to us.

It is from the mother that the little child receives the answer to this prayer. "God could not be everywhere present, and therefore he made mothers," said the old rabbis. Teachers come after our mothers as the guides of our youth. Then all through the days God reveals himself in the lives of those who touch us with their love and influence us through their wisdom and goodness. In the olden days angels came to tell men what God would have them do. No doubt they come yet, ministering unseen and unheard, whispering in our ears many a suggestion which sets our feet in safe and right paths. Yet there are human angels,—for angels are only God's messengers, those whom he sends. Beautifully does Mrs. Sangster say,—

> "But in these days I know my angels well;
>   They brush my garments on the common way,
> They take my hand and very softly tell
>   Some bit of comfort in the waning day.
>
> "And though their angel names I do not ken,
>   Though in their faces human want I read,
> They are God-given in this world of men,
>   God-sent to bless it in its hours of need."

Our wise, good, and true human friends are God's angels to us. They are sent in answer to our prayer that God would cause us to know the way wherein we should walk. They teach us and give us the wise counsel which directs us in the heavenward path.

God answers our prayer also in his providences. One day after you have prayed your morning prayer you are sent in from your busy life, to lie down on a sick-bed; probably you do not think of this as God's answer to your request to be shown the way; but is it not so? Your path leads into the shadows, and you must suffer a while. No doubt this is the right way. You are learning some lesson that you could not have learned out in the crowded street, in the open field, or in the busy mart.

There are certain song-birds which are taught new songs by being shut up for a time in the darkness. Another bird with the song that is to be learned is brought and placed near the little prisoner, where it sings its sweet notes over and over. The bird in the darkness listens, catches the song, learns it; and when it is taken out into the light, it knows the new song and sings it everywhere. So God ofttimes takes his children into the darkness that he may teach them some song they would not learn in the busy world. In the shadows of the sick-room they hear the sweet things they are to learn.

17

Comfort they had never known before breaks out as in strains of heavenly music from old familiar Bible texts which they had conned from childhood. Friends come and tell them precious things about the love and grace of God, and sing hymns of faith and hope in their quiet chamber. The Spirit of God whispers in their ears the things of Christ. After all this experience, the curtain is drawn and these children of God go out into the world to sing in the light the songs they have learned in the darkness.

This from Jean Paul Richter: "'Ah!' said the imprisoned bird, 'how unhappy were I in my eternal night, but for those melodious tones which sometimes make their way to me like beams of light from afar, and cheer my gloomy day! But I will myself repeat those heavenly melodies like an echo, until I have stamped them in my heart, and then I shall be able to bring comfort to myself in my darkness.' Thus spoke the little warbler, and soon had learned the sweet airs that were sung to it with voice and instrument. That done, the curtain was raised; for the darkness had been purposely contrived to assist in its instruction."

Life is full of these strange answers to our morning prayer, "Cause me to know the way wherein I should walk." Sometimes a sore disappointment comes, or a keen sorrow, or a misfortune, as we call it, seeing but the earthly side and the beginning of the experience. Our plans are rudely set aside. Our hopes are laid in the dust. "Surely this is not the way," we say. Yet why should we doubt that it is so, when we have asked our Father to cause us to know the way? Shall we not rather sweetly accept the guidance, believing that the path in which we are led is the right one?

If Joseph had prayed this prayer the morning he left home to go on the errand to his brothers, he might have wondered on his way to Egypt, as a slave, if that were the answer. But as the years went on he learned that there had been no mistake that day. If he had escaped from his brothers or from the caravan, he would have only spoiled one of God's thoughts of love for him. So it is always, when we put our hand in God's and trust him. He may lead us through valleys of shadows, but beyond the gloom we shall come to green pastures. It is safe, as we go out into the unopened day, to pray, "Cause me to know the way wherein I should walk."

> "I pray
> But this: Let every day
> Be modelled still
> By thine own hand; my will
> Be only thine, however deep
> I have to bend, thy hand to keep.
> Let me not simply do, but be content,
> Sure that the little crosses each are sent,
> And no mistake can ever be,
> With thine own hand to choose for me."

III. TO BE KEPT FROM EVIL.

The third petition of this morning prayer is, "Deliver me, O Lord, from mine enemies: I flee unto thee to hide me." The day is full of dangers,—dangers we cannot see, and from which we cannot protect ourselves. Disease lurks in the air we breathe, and hides in the water we drink, or in the food we eat. Along the street where we walk, on the railway over which we ride, there are perils. Any moment we may be stricken down. There may be enemies who are plotting against us, conspiring to do us harm.

There certainly are spiritual enemies who are seeking to destroy us. The sunniest **day** is full of them. No African jungle is so full of wild beasts, savage and blood-thirsty, as are the common days in our lives of spiritual enemies and perils. We are aware of no danger, and hence cannot protect ourselves.

What, then, can we do? As we go out in the morning we càn offer this prayer: "Deliver me, O Lord, from mine enemies: I flee unto thee to hide me." We can thus put our frail, imperilled lives into the hands of the mighty God.

We are not promised that our prayers shall take the perils and temptations out of our day. It is not thus that God usually helps. We are bidden to cast our burden upon the Lord, but we are not told that he will lift it away from us. The promise is that we shall be sustained and strengthened in bearing it. We need the burden. It is God's gift to us, and has a blessing in it which we cannot afford to miss. Prayer does not take our trials away, but it puts our life into the hands of God, so that in his keeping we shall be kept from harm while we. pass through the trials. It brings God's love about us as an atmosphere, God's grace into our heart to preserve us from doubt, from fear, from falling into sin, and God's strength into our life that we may be victorious over our enemies.

Not to pray as we go into the day's dangers and trials is to meet them without the help of Christ, and surely to suffer hurt, possibly to fall. A writer says, " A sorrow comes upon you. Omit prayer, and you fall out of God's testing into the devil's temptation; you get angry, hard of heart, reckless. But meet the dreadful hour with prayer, cast your care on God, claim him as your Father, though he seem cruel, and the degrading, paralyzing, embittering effects of pain and sorrow pass away; a stream of sanctifying and softening thought pours into the soul, and that which might have wrought your fall but works in you the peaceable fruits of righteousness."

There are some people who omit private prayer in the morning, praying only in the evening. But how can any one safely go out to meet the perils and evils of all kinds which lie hidden in the sunshine of the fairest, quietest day, without having first committed the keeping of his life to God? A young girl recently told how that one morning, being late and hurried, she did not offer her usual prayer before leaving her room. After she had gone to her work, her little brother, who slept in the same room with his sister, came to his mother, evidently much distressed about something. He told her that Alice had not said her prayer that morning before she went to work, adding, "I'm afraid something will happen to her to-day." Then, after a moment's thoughtful pause, he said, "I'm going to say her prayer for her." And the little, loving intercessor fell on his knees beside his mother's chair and made an earnest, tender prayer for the sister who had forgotten that morning to pray for herself. The child felt that there were dangers in the great world, amid which his sister would not be safe that day, unless the hand of prayer had drawn the divine shelter down about her.

If we understood what perils there are for us in any common day, if our eyes were opened that we might have a glimpse of the enemies that wait for us in cloud and sunshine, we would never dare to go forth from our door any morning until we had asked God to keep us from harm and deliver us from evil.

IV. TO BE TAUGHT TO DO GOD'S WILL.

The fourth petition of this morning prayer is, "Teach me to do thy will; for thou art my God: thy spirit is good; lead me in the land of uprightness." A little earlier the prayer was, "Cause me to know the way wherein I should walk." But knowing the way is not enough; we must also walk in it. Mary Lyon said she feared nothing so much as that she should not know all her duty, and that she should not do it. When we ask God in the morning to show us the way, we must ask him also to teach us to go in the right path. "Teach me to do thy will; . . . lead me in the land of uprightness." A great many people know their duty and do not do it. Perhaps none of us do all the duty we know. Indeed, none of us do all that we sincerely intend to do. At the best, our performance falls below our ideal.

While the spirit is willing, the flesh is weak, and therefore we blunder and come short in our holiest endeavors. Our clumsy hands mar the lovely ideals which our souls vision. It is not enough that we be taught what we ought to do; we need to add the prayer, "Teach me

24

to do thy will." Our hearts are not inclined to do the things that are right. It is not easy to be good. The tide sets ever against us. We need to be taught and trained and led with strong hand in the way of God's commandments. We do not go far in the path of holiness until we find that we must be saved almost in spite of ‑ ourselves. St. Paul's seventh of Romans' experience is soon discovered to be a very common one in earnest Christian living. "Not what I would, that do I practise; but what I hate, that I do. . . . to will is present with me, but to do that which is good is not. For the good which I would I do not: but the evil which I would not, that I practise."

Yet we are not to despair of learning the lesson of true and holy living because we find it hard, even impossible, to unhelped human nature. Nothing is impossible to the grace of God. If the gospel of love only caused us to know the way in which we should walk, we might despair, for alone we never could walk in this way, however well we might know it. But the gospel does more: it also teaches us how to walk, how to attain the beauty that seems so hard to attain.

The little child has feet, but it does not know how to use them. The time comes when it must learn to walk. The mother begins to teach it. The lesson must be learned slowly. It is not enough to tell the child what it is expected to do, or to explain to it the way men and women walk, or to show it an example of good walking. The little feet lack both strength and skill for the exercise. The wise mother sets about teaching her child how to walk. She tries first to get it to take a single step, and then two steps, and patiently trains it until by and by the child can walk and run easily at will. So must we be taught to walk in God's ways. We have to learn in short, easy lessons, one step, and then another, and then another, until at length we can walk and not be weary, and run and not faint.

How is this prayer answered? In what way does God teach us how to do his will? First, he sets the lessons for us in the Scriptures. Our morning Bible reading gives us a copy, as when a scholar is given a clean white page with a beautifully written or engraved copy at the top of it. He is to try to write on the lines of the page like the copy. If he is only

a beginner, his writing falls far short of the
beautiful top line. But if he is diligent and
faithful, the successive lines show evidence, at
least, of striving to learn. Our text for the
day is the copy set for us. It is, for example,
"Bear ye one another's burdens, and so fulfil
the law of Christ." Naturally we are selfish,
and think only of ourselves. We are not dis-
posed to give much thought to others. We
are quite apt to pass by on the other side
when we see one who is in some trouble or
need. At least, we are not likely to stop to
help our neighbors carry their loads. But as we
go out in the morning with our bit of Bible
lesson in mind and heart, intent on letting it
into our life, we soon begin to find that we
cannot give our undivided attention to our-
selves. Our text stands by us like an angel
mentor, sharply reminding us at almost every
step that here and here and here are over-
burdened ones whom we must try to help a
little with their load.

One such new lesson set for us every morn-
ing will keep us ever learning how to live, how
to do God's will. We cannot learn our lessons
in any one day, for they are long; but if we

are earnest and diligent, we shall always be at
school and shall be continually advancing in
our spiritual education. Then, while we apply
ourselves to our lessons we have the help of
the divine Spirit. There is a beautiful legend of
Michael Angelo which illustrates this. Once the
great artist was overwrought and very weary,
and while his picture was yet incomplete he fell
asleep. The rest of the story is told in a little
poem:

" Then an angel came, and very featly
   Seized the brush and made the canvas living;
While a sort of music sounded sweetly,
   Deeper slumber to the artist giving.

" There the loving angel toiled and tarried
   Till the sunlight failed and day had fleeted;
Wrought the wondrous work, a love-thought carried
   Into colors fit and fair-completed."

It is only a legend, but its lesson is true.
When we strive to learn our lessons, doing our
best to put upon the canvas of our life the
beautiful things of God's thought and will, and
when we grow weary,—not of, but in, our effort,
—God's angels come and finish our work while
we sleep. In faith and love we may go forth,

morning by morning, praying, "Teach me to do thy will; for thou art my God."

V. LIFE FOR THE DAY.

The fifth petition of this morning prayer is, "Quicken me, O Lord, for thy name's sake." We have no strength for the duties and conflicts of the day. Life is too hard for us. Its burdens are heavier than we can bear. Its duties are too serious for our unaided wisdom. Its sorrows would break our heart if no divine help or comfort came. Our life is too scant in its own fountains; we must have God.

No one is ready to go forth into any common day until he has received divine quickening. And this is promised to every one who will seek it. It comes in many ways. You are in sorrow, and, opening the Bible, you read words of comfort. As you read and believe, there comes into your soul a blessing of strength and peace, and you are strangely comforted. Or you are entering into a temptation. You have no strength of your own to meet it. Again there comes a word of Scripture with its promise of help, and with the word comes

strength which nerves your heart, and you are
more than conqueror through Christ.

> "I asked for strength; for with the noontide heat
> I fainted, while the reapers, singing sweet,
> Went forward with ripe sheaves I could not bear.
> Then came the Master, with his blood-stained feet,
> And lifted me with sympathetic care.
> Then on his arm I leaned till all was done,
> And I stood with the rest, at set of sun,
>   My task complete."

VI. DELIVERANCE FROM TROUBLE.

The last petition of this wonderful morning
prayer is, "In thy righteousness bring my soul
out of trouble." We can never plan our life
so as to miss sorrow. Indeed, the ministry of
pain is indispensable in human life. "Gardeners,
sometimes, when they would bring a rose to
richer blooming, deprive it for a season of light
and moisture. Silent and dark it stands, dropping
one fading leaf after another, and seeming to go
patiently down to death. But when every leaf
is dropped and the plant stands stripped to the
uttermost, a new life is seen then working in
the buds, from which shall spring a tenderer

foliage and a brighter wealth of flowers. So, often, in celestial gardening, every leaf of earthly joy must drop before a new and divine bloom visits the soul."

Thus it is that sorrow itself works blessing and good in the believer when he is truly in communion with Christ. Deliverance from the trouble is not always granted: ofttimes this would not be a kindness; it would be the taking away of a rich blessing. We are not delivered from it, but in it we are kept from all harm, and receive good instead.

> "All those who journey, soon or late,
>   Must pass within the garden's gate;
>   Must kneel alone in darkness there
>   And battle with some fierce despair.
>   God pity those who cannot say,
>   'Not mine, but thine;' who only pray,
>   'Let this cup pass,' and cannot see
>   The purpose in Gethsemane."

Such is this old-time morning prayer for a busy or troubled week-day. It is as appropriate for us as it was for those who centuries ago breathed out its words and found their day made safe and bright by the protection, the grace, and the love of Christ.

The daily morning prayer used by Dr. Arnold, of Rugby, is one which all busy people might well make their own: "O Lord, I have a busy world around me; eye, ear, and thought will be needed for all my work to be done in this busy world. Now, ere I enter on it, I would commit eye and ear and thought to thee. Do thou bless them, and keep their work thine, that as through thy natural laws my heart beats, and my blood flows, without any thought of mine, so my spiritual life may hold on its course at these times when my mind cannot consciously turn to thee to commit each particular thought to thy service. Hear my prayer for my dear Redeemer's sake. Amen."

CPSIA information can be obtained
at www.ICGtesting.com
Printed in the USA
BVHW04s0012250718
522489BV00012B/254/P